SING THE FAITH

The Presence of
GOD

SUSAN CHERWIEN

Augsburg Fortress
PUBLISHERS

SING THE FAITH

The Presence of
GOD

SUSAN CHERWIEN

Editors:
Vicky Goplin,
Victor Jortack,
Elizabeth Drotning
Cover design:
Marti Naughton

Scripture quotations
are from New Revised
Standard Version
Bible, copyright
© 1989 Division of
Christian Education
of the National
Council of the
Churches of Christ in
the United States of
America. Used by
permission.

INTRODUCTION

Welcome to Sing the Faith!

Welcome to *The Presence of God,* one of three volumes in the Sing the Faith Bible Study series. You are embarking on a biblical exploration of grace through the poetry, music, and history of five of the most beloved hymns of the Christian tradition.

Hymns are the faith people sing. The lyrics are owned by the people as the fabric of their theology. Many hymns have been in the memories of churchgoers for years. The melodies and texts of hymns are often retained after most other memory has faded. This series will allow participants to connect these well-loved hymns to biblical texts.

Pastors and worship leaders spend a significant amount of time searching for hymns related to the Sunday readings, the theme, and the mood of each service. Indexes are available to assist planners in coordinating biblical texts and songs. The Sing the Faith series brings this information and its powerful faith formation capability to you.

Each session focuses on one hymn. Participants will reflect on their personal history with the hymn, explore biblical connections in the texts, learn the history and legends associated with the hymn, and consider how the message of the hymn applies to their daily journey of faith.

Preparing your study

The Sing the Faith series, designed for small-group Bible study, encourages interaction among participants to help them grow and enrich their journeys of faith. Alternate groupings, with minor modifications, would be possible. Individuals might use this resource for personal study or partner with another individual to study and correspond by phone or e-mail.

The thematically connected hymns in each volume can be studied at any time and in any church season. The five-week structure makes this an ideal choice during the season of Lent.

The material is planned for weekly gatherings. The meeting place could be at church or in homes. The key will be finding a place where everyone can feel safe as they share, reflect, and pray together.

This study is ideal for rotational leadership. As leaders and participants discover increased connection between worship and study, the understanding of leadership will continue to broaden. If a pastor is a part of your group, include him or her in the rotation. The opportunity to operate as a participant will be welcomed.

Adults of all ages and stages will find this study useful—singles groups, men's breakfasts, mom's time out, and new member study are just a few ideas. Because of the universality of the hymns used in this series, a young adult group may be as vital as an older adult group.

Planning each session

Gathering for the story

The first three pages of each session introduce the hymn. The instructions invite you to transition from a time of fellowship as you arrive, to gathering your thoughts about the hymn, checking in with each other, and then experiencing the hymn (see page 6), and finally prayer together.

Learning the story

This section provides relevant information about the text, the tune, and the legends of each hymn. The intent is not in-depth study, but an opportunity to discover stories and anecdotes about the persons and circumstances that were a part of the creation of the hymn.

Our story

Hymns and songs carry emotional and cognitive memories. In this section, you will be asked to reflect on how the hymn has been part of your growth in the Christian faith. The questions, similar in all sessions, provide time and a safe opportunity to share how the music and poetry has affected who we are as believers.

The biblical story

Unless the hymn writer indicated a specific biblical passage, the intended textual connection can never be certain. The writer of this study discovered textual connections and images for one stanza of each hymn and has provided questions to help you search for personal meaning related to faith traditions and the Bible.

Texts were selected from the New Revised Standard Version of the Bible (NRSV), but each participant may use his or her own Bible. Using a variety of translations can bring new perspectives to your discussions.

Additional questions to reflect on in this section of the study are:

◆ What is normally taken for granted about this passage?

◆ What is related to your own journey of faith?

◆ What connections to biblical and doctrinal understanding do you find?

◆ What may affect you personally in this text?

Living the story

Each hymn ends with three questions addressing how this hymn will affect the way you live your faith as a result of your learning. What message will you bring to each day?

Each session ends with praying and singing. The closing prayer, with time for individual petitions, and singing weave new dimensions to the hymn's familiar words and images.

Experiencing the hymn

An important part of this study is the experience of singing. Whether your group is large or small, raise your voices together each week. If a piano and accompanist are available, look for the full score in your favorite hymnal. All hymns are included in *Lutheran Book of Worship* or *With One Voice*, as well as in most traditional Christian hymnals.

If your group has instrumentalists, invite them to play with you as you sing. Perhaps someone's hidden talent will shine! Invite a young person or two from your congregation who play in their school orchestra or band to play along for one session.

Many of the hymns in the Sing the Faith volumes appear on numerous recordings. The reference list on page 47 offers a starting place for your search. You might publicize your study in your church newsletter or bulletin by listing the hymns and asking for recording recommendations. In addition, piano collections that include one or more of the hymns are suggested on this page.

Whether you sing *a cappella* or with a pipe organ at its fullest, enjoy your time with the music, with the texts, with memories of the past and hope for the future, and with each other as together you Sing the Faith.

GREAT IS THY FAITHFULNESS

1 Great is thy faith-ful-ness, O God my Fa-ther; there is no
2 Sum-mer and win-ter and spring-time and har-vest, sun, moon, and
3 Par-don for sin and a peace that en-dur-eth, thine own dear

shad-ow of turn-ing with thee; thou chang-est not, thy com-
stars in their cours-es a-bove join with all na-ture in
pres-ence to cheer and to guide; strength for to-day and bright

pas-sions, they fail not; as thou hast been, thou for-ev-er wilt be.
man-i-fold wit-ness to thy great faith-ful-ness, mer-cy, and love.
hope for to-mor-row, bless-ings all mine, with ten thou-sand be-side!

Refrain

Great is thy faith-ful-ness! Great is thy faith-ful-ness! Morn-ing by

morn-ing new mer-cies I see; all I have need-ed thy

hand hath pro-vid-ed; great is thy faith-ful-ness, Lord, un-to me.

Text: Thomas O. Chisholm, 1866–1960
Music: FAITHFULNESS, William M. Runyan, 1870–1957

Great Is Thy Faithfulness ◆ 7

GATHERING FOR THE STORY

Greet participants as they arrive. Invite them to record their responses to this question in their book.

A Bible concordance would be a helpful tool for people who want to list text citations or search for stories by key words.

Begin with introductions. Ask volunteers to share the stories they selected, then say the prayer together.

Invite the group to sing "Great is Thy Faithfulness" (see page 6). Since this hymn is well suited to four-part singing, encourage participants who are able to sing the choral parts.

(10 minutes)

When you think of God's faithfulness, what Bible stories come to mind?

Blessed are you, O Lord our God,
for your love is with us in all hours and all seasons.
Blessed are you, for your love does not change.
Bless now, we pray, this time of study and of song,
that we may be renewed in our love for you
    and all that you have made,
for you are God forever and ever. Amen

GREAT IS THY FAITHFULNESS

Great is thy faithfulness, O God my Father;
there is no shadow of turning with thee;
thou changest not, thy compassions, they fail not;
as thou hast been, thou forever wilt be.

Refrain *Great is thy faithfulness!*
Great is thy faithfulness!
Morning by morning new mercies I see;
all I have needed thy hand hath provided;
great is thy faithfulness, Lord, unto me!

Summer and winter and springtime and harvest,
sun, moon, and stars in their courses above
join with all nature in manifold witness
to thy great faithfulness, mercy, and love. *Refrain*

Pardon for sin and a peace that endureth,
thine own dear presence to cheer and to guide;
strength for today and bright hope for tomorrow,
blessings all mine, with ten thousand beside! *Refrain*

Thomas O. Chisholm, 1866-1960

LEARNING THE STORY

After participants read the hymn background, talk about information they found meaningful or helpful.
(5 minutes)

The text

Thomas Obediah Chisholm was born on a small farm in Franklin, Kentucky in 1866. At age 27, after time as a schoolteacher and a journalist, he became a Methodist minister. He based "Great Is Thy Faithfulness" on Lamentations 3:19-24 and sent it to William Runyon, his good friend. During his lifetime, Chisholm wrote about 1,200 hymn texts. He died in Ocean Grove, New Jersey, in 1960.

The tune

William Marion Runyon (1870-1957) was a lifelong friend of Thomas Chisholm. He was already a church organist at age 12, and in 1891 was ordained as a minister in the Methodist church. From 1925 to 1948 he served as music editor and advisor for Hope Publishing. This tune is named FAITHFULNESS.

The legend

"Great Is Thy Faithfulness" was published in 1923, along with several other Chisholm texts, in the collection *Songs of Salvation and Service*. Runyon said of this work, "This particular poem held such an appeal that I prayed most earnestly that my tune might carry its message in a worthy way, and the subsequent history of its use indicates that God answered prayer."

"Great Is Thy Faithfulness" has become the unofficial school hymn of the Moody Bible Institute in Chicago.

OUR STORY

When was the first time you heard this hymn?
What do you recall about that event?

You may need to adapt these questions for the participants in your group. Ask them to record their responses and then share their stories.
(10 minutes)

What personal memories do you associate with this hymn?

What does this hymn say to you?

THE BIBLICAL STORY

Invite participants to find the passages in their Bibles and record responses to the questions.

Great is thy faithfulness
Lamentations 3:19-24

What personal qualities does it take to sing the words of verses 22-23 of the Lamentations text in the face of such destruction?

The book of Lamentations was written after the Babylonians leveled Jerusalem in 586-87 BCE.

How would you describe the hymn writer's view of God? How does this compare with your view of God?

There is no shadow of turning with thee
James 1:17

What does it mean for your life that God does not change? Can you think of times when the faithfulness of God sustained you?

Thou changest not
Malachi 3:6

Do you think God ever changes?

Determine if your group would prefer to:

◆ read and respond to all passages and questions before talking

◆ read, respond, and discuss one passage at a time

(20 minutes)

Morning by morning new mercies I see
Lamentations 3:22-23

What new mercies do you see each morning?
What can you do to recognize new mercies each day?

LIVING THE STORY

Invite participants to reflect for a few moments on today's conversation, and then respond to the questions. It is important to share the responses to these questions, so your group can offer prayer support to each other throughout the week.

Select a leader for your next meeting and remind everyone of the time and location.

Close by singing "Great is Thy Faithfulness" and praying together.

(10 minutes)

What does this hymn say to you at this time in your life?

How does this hymn affect the way you live each day?

Are there specific times this week when you might live your response to this hymn?

O faithful God, your mercy and your compassion
hold and sustain us.
We praise you for the gift of your faithful love.
We thank you for the blessing
of your loving presence.
May we be renewed each day
    by the study of your word,
renewed each morning
    by the knowledge of your mercy.
Call to mind your faithful people,
    and give ear to our individual prayers.
Silence for reflection.
For you are God, faithful to all ages of ages.
Amen

WHAT A FELLOWSHIP, WHAT A JOY DIVINE

1 What a   fel - low-ship, what a   joy di - vine, lean-ing on the ev - er - last-ing arms;
2 Oh, how sweet to walk   in   this pil-grim way, lean-ing on the ev - er - last-ing arms;
3 What have I   to dread, what have I   to   fear, lean-ing on the ev - er - last-ing arms;

what a   bless - ed - ness, what   a   peace is mine, lean-ing on the ev-er-last-ing arms.
oh, how bright the path grows from day to day, lean-ing on the ev-er-last-ing arms.
I   have bless - ed peace with my Lord so near, lean-ing on the ev-er-last-ing arms.

Refrain

Lean - ing,   lean - ing,   safe and se-cure from   all   a - larms;

lean - ing,   lean - ing,   lean - ing on   the ev - er - last - ing   arms.

Text: Elisha Hoffman, 1839–1929
Music: SHOWALTER, Anthony J. Showalter, 1858–1924

GATHERING FOR THE STORY

Greet participants as they arrive. Invite them to record their response to this question in their book.

Consider playing a quiet, comforting instrumental recording as people are writing.

Be sure participants know each other's names. Ask volunteers to talk about some of the experiences they noted, then say the prayer together.

Invite the group to sing "What a Fellowship, What a Joy Divine" (see page 6). Encourage participants who are able to sing the four-part harmony gospel-style.

(10 minutes)

What times do you remember when you felt frightened and were comforted by the arms of someone?

O God, our Refuge, you have promised
    to comfort and care for your people.
May we always feel your loving arms supporting us.
May we always be guided by the sure sense
    of your comforting presence.
Open our hearts to your word.
Open our minds to your wisdom,
    that we may grow in fellowship with you
    and with each other.
Amen

WHAT A FELLOWSHIP, WHAT A JOY DIVINE

What a fellowship, what a joy divine,
leaning on the everlasting arms;
what a blessedness, what a peace is mine,
leaning on the everlasting arms.

Refrain *Leaning, leaning,*
safe and secure from all alarms;
leaning, leaning,
leaning on the everlasting arms.

Oh, how sweet to walk in this pilgrim way,
leaning on the everlasting arms;
oh, how bright the path grows from day to day,
leaning on the everlasting arms. *Refrain*

What have I to dread, what have I to fear,
leaning on the everlasting arms;
I have blessed peace with my Lord so near,
leaning on the everlasting arms. *Refrain*

Text: Elisha Hoffman, 1839-1929

LEARNING THE STORY

After participants read the hymn background, talk about information they found meaningful or helpful.
(5 minutes)

The text

The stanzas for "What a Fellowship, What a Joy Divine" were written by Elisha Albright Hoffman (1839-1927), author of more than 1,000 gospel hymns. Born in Orwigsburg, Pennsylvania, the son of an evangelical minister, he received his education at Union Bible Seminary and served with the 47th Pennsylvania Infantry Division in the Civil War. He was the first music editor for Hope Publishing (1894-1912).

The tune

Anthony Johnson Showalter (1858-1924) began musical training with his father, who was active in the singing school movement. Singing schools taught children the basics of sight-singing and music reading through the repeated singing of hymns written in shape-notes, in which each note of the scale was written on a musical staff and had a distinctively shaped notehead such as a square or triangle. He founded the AJ Showalter Company, authoring 60 books on teaching music and producing many more volumes. The tune, SHOWALTER, is in the style of shape-note hymns.

The legend

Upon hearing two former students had lost their wives, Showalter responded to them with letters citing Deuteronomy 33:27, "The eternal God is thy refuge, and underneath are the everlasting arms" (King James Version). Further reflection led him to write the tune, the setting, and the refrain. He asked his friend Elisha Hoffman to complete the stanzas. First published in 1887 in *The Glad Evangel for Revival, Camp and Evangelistic Meetings*, it is also known as "Leaning on the Everlasting Arms."

OUR STORY

When was the first time you heard this hymn?
What do you recall about that time?

You may need to adapt these questions for the participants in your group. Ask them to record their responses and then share their stories. *(10 minutes)*

What personal memories do you associate with this hymn?

What does this hymn say to you?

THE BIBLICAL STORY

Invite participants to find the passages in their Bibles and record responses to the questions.

At this point in Deuteronomy, Moses is blessing the tribes of Israel before his death. The wandering nation has not yet crossed over the Jordan River into Canaan. Yet Moses concludes his blessing with words that speak of God's having already accomplished what God had promised.

Leaning on the everlasting arms
Deuteronomy 33:26-29

Why do you think this might be significant?

What might this mean for our lives?

What a joy divine
Psalm16:7-11

How does joy differ from happiness?

What a peace is mine
Psalm 46

Does catastrophe befall the followers of God?

Determine if your group would prefer to:
♦ read and respond to all passages and questions before talking

♦ read, respond, and discuss one passage at a time

(20 minutes)

What is the source of a sense of peace?

Safe and secure from all alarms
Psalm 27:1-5

What shall we fear? How can we set aside fears?

LIVING THE STORY

Invite participants to reflect for a few moments on today's conversation, then respond to the questions. It is important to share the responses to these questions, so your group can offer prayer support to each other throughout the week.

Select a leader for your next meeting and remind everyone of the time and location.

Close by singing "What a Fellowship, What a Joy Divine" and praying together.

(10 minutes)

What does this hymn say to you at this time in your life?

How does this hymn affect the way you live each day?

Are there specific times this week when you might live your response to this hymn?

O God, our dwelling place, you have blessed us
   with your everlasting presence.
You have lifted us up and held us in your arms.
Abide with us as we leave this place.
Bless us, so that we may comfort and console
   the frightened and the lost.
Hear the prayers of your people.
Silence for reflection.
Send us out now in peace and joy
   to the glory of your holy name.
Amen

BLESSED ASSURANCE

1 Bless-ed as-sur-ance, Je-sus is mine! Oh, what a fore-taste of glo-ry di-vine!
2 Per-fect sub-mis-sion, per-fect de-light, vi-sions of rap-ture now burst on my sight;
3 Per-fect sub-mis-sion, all is at rest; I in my Sav-ior am hap-py and blest,

Heir of sal-va-tion, pur-chase of God, born of his Spir-it, washed in his blood.
an-gels de-scend-ing bring from a-bove ech-oes of mer-cy, whis-pers of love.
watch-ing and wait-ing, look-ing a-bove, filled with his good-ness, lost in his love.

Refrain

This is my sto-ry, this is my song, prais-ing my Sav-ior all the day long:

this is my sto-ry, this is my song, prais-ing my Sav-ior all the day long.

Text: Fanny J. Crosby, 1820–1915
Music: ASSURANCE, Phoebe P. Knapp, 1830–1908

GATHERING FOR THE STORY

Greet participants as they arrive. Invite them to record their responses to this question in their book.

How many ways can you think of to praise God?

Begin with introductions. Ask volunteers to share their ideas, and then say the prayer together.

Invite the group to sing "Blessed Assurance" (see page 6). This hymn is well suited to four-part singing. Encourage participants who are able to harmonize.

(10 minutes)

Glory to you, O God, for through Christ Jesus
you have made us heirs of salvation.
Through your Spirit you have brought us to new life.
Through your grace you have given us
a foretaste of blessed life in your presence.
Be with us now as we study, pray, and praise,
that we may be filled with the assurance
of your love and care.
In your name we pray.
Amen

BLESSED ASSURANCE

Blessed assurance, Jesus is mine!
Oh, what a foretaste of glory divine!
Heir of salvation, purchase of God,
born of his Spirit, washed in his blood.

Refrain *This is my story, this is my song,*
praising my Savior, all the day long:
this is my story, this is my song,
praising my Savior all the day long.

Perfect submission, perfect delight,
visions of rapture now burst on my sight;
angels descending bring from above
echoes of mercy, whispers of love. *Refrain*

Perfect submission, all is at rest;
I in my Savior am happy and blest,
watching and waiting, looking above,
filled with his goodness, lost in his love. *Refrain*

Text: Fanny J. Crosby, 1820-1915

LEARNING THE STORY

After participants read the hymn background, talk about information they found meaningful or helpful.
(5 minutes)

The text

"Blessed Assurance" is one of the most beloved of the nearly 8,000 hymn texts written by Fanny Crosby. Born in 1823, she lost her eyesight at the age of six weeks. She taught English grammar, rhetoric, and Roman and American history at the New York City Institute for the Blind from 1847 to 1858. Fanny Crosby wrote under as many as 216 different pseudonyms and sets of initials, including Ella Dale, Jenny V., Mrs. Kate Grinley, and Miss Viola, and could recite from memory the first four books of the Torah and the four gospels. At one point, she was under contract to write three hymns a week for one of her publishers. She died in 1915 at the age of 95.

The tune

The tune ASSURANCE was composed by Phoebe P. Knapp, daughter of the evangelist Dr. Walter Palmer and his wife Phoebe. Born in 1839, daughter Phoebe showed musical talent quite early in life and eventually composed more than 500 gospel hymns. Phoebe died suddenly in 1908, shortly after receiving a visit from her longtime friend Fanny Crosby.

The legend

Until 1955, nothing marked the grave of Fanny Crosby except a small marble marker with the words "Aunt Fanny" and "She hath done what she could." On May 1, 1955, the citizens of Bridgeport, Connecticut, erected a large marble marker on her grave to honor the "Queen of the Gospel Hymn" and inscribed the stone with the first stanza of "Blessed Assurance."

OUR STORY

When did you hear this hymn for the first time?
What do you recall about that time?

You may need to adapt these questions for the participants in your group. Ask them to record their responses and then share their stories. *(10 minutes)*

What personal memories do you associate with this hymn?

What does this hymn say to you?

THE BIBLICAL STORY

Invite participants to find the passages in their Bibles and record responses to the questions.

Blessed assurance
Hebrews 11:1

How can one have assurance in what is not seen?

Jesus is mine
John 17:20-23

How does this phrase feel true for you?

Heir of salvation
Titus 3:6-7

How do you think we inherit salvation?

Purchase of God
1 Corinthians 6:19-20

Why have we been purchased by God?

Born of his Spirit
John 3:5-8

What do you think it means to be born of the Spirit?

Determine if your group would prefer to:

◆ read and respond to all passages and questions before talking

◆ read, respond, and discuss one passage at a time

(20 minutes)

Washed in his blood
Revelation 7:13-14

What does this image mean for you and what feeling does it evoke?

Praising my Savior all the day long
Psalm 34:1

How do you find yourself responding to God's good grace toward you?

LIVING THE STORY

Invite participants to reflect for a few moments on today's conversation, then respond to the questions. It is important to share the responses to these questions, so your group can offer prayer support to each other throughout the week.

Select a leader for your next meeting and remind everyone of the time and location.

Close by singing "Blessed Assurance" and praying together.

(10 minutes)

What does this hymn say to you at this time in your life?

How does this hymn affect the way you live each day?

Are there specific times this week when you might live your response to this hymn?

God of blessing, God of glory,
we praise you for the blessed assurance
    of your love shown to us in Jesus Christ.
We praise you with our story and with our song.
You have gathered us together as your people.
Hear our earnest prayers.
Silence for reflection.
Send us out with lives full of praise,
    blessed and blessing as we go
    about our daily lives,
for you are God, forever and ever. Amen

IMMORTAL, INVISIBLE, GOD ONLY WISE

1. Im - mor - tal, in - vis - i - ble, God on - ly wise,
in light in - ac - ces - si - ble hid from our eyes,
most bless - ed, most glo - rious, the An - cient of Days,
al - might - y, vic - to - rious, thy great name we praise!

2. Un - rest - ing, un - hast - ing, and si - lent as light,
nor want - ing, nor wast - ing, thou rul - est in might;
thy jus - tice like moun - tains high soar - ing a - bove
thy clouds which are foun - tains of good - ness and love.

3. To all, life thou giv - est, to both great and small;
in all life thou liv - est, the true life of all;
we blos - som and flour - ish like leaves on the tree,
and with - er and per - ish, but naught chang - eth thee.

4. Thou reign - est in glo - ry; thou dwell - est in light;
thine an - gels a - dore thee, all veil - ing their sight;
all laud we would ren - der; oh, help us to see
'tis on - ly the splen - dor of light hid - eth thee!

Text: Walter Chalmers Smith, 1824–1903, alt.
Music: ST. DENIO, Welsh folk tune

GATHERING FOR THE STORY

Greet participants as they arrive. Invite them to record their responses to this question in their book.

Begin with introductions. Ask volunteers to share their reactions, and then say the prayer together.

Invite the group to sing "Immortal, Invisible" (see page 6). If someone in your group plays a brass instrument, invite him or her to play as you sing.

(10 minutes)

Have you ever experienced an overwhelming sense of the presence of God?

Immortal God, glorious in light,
we praise you for your splendor,
    your wisdom, your truth.
Open our eyes, enlighten our minds,
    and guide us to your truth,
that all our days might be filled
    with the wonder of your glory.
Amen

IMMORTAL, INVISIBLE, GOD ONLY WISE

Immortal, invisible, God only wise,
in light inaccessible hid from our eyes,
most blessed, most glorious, the Ancient of Days,
almighty, victorious, thy great name we praise!

Unresting, unhasting, and silent as light,
nor wanting, nor wasting, thou rulest in might;
thy justice like mountains high soaring above
thy clouds which are fountains of goodness and love.

To all, life thou givest, to both great and small;
in all life thou livest, the true life of all;
we blossom and flourish like leaves on the tree,
and wither and perish, but naught changeth thee.

Thou reignest in glory; thou dwellest in light;
thine angels adore thee, all veiling their sight;
all laud we would render; oh, help us to see
'tis only the splendor of light hideth thee!

Text: Walter Chalmers Smith, 1824-1903, alt.

LEARNING THE STORY

After participants read the hymn background, talk about information they found meaningful or helpful.
(5 minutes)

The text

An ordained pastor of the Scottish Free Church (Presbyterian), Walter Chalmers Smith wrote a number of poetic works that were published during his lifetime (1824-1908). He was born in Aberdeen, Scotland, and educated at the University of Aberdeen and New College, Edinburgh. In 1876, he published *Hymns of Christ and the Christian Life*, which included the hymn "Immortal, Invisible." He died in Kinbuck, Perthshire, in 1908.

The tune

The hymn tune ST. DENIO was composed in 1859 by Ieuan Qwyllt. It was based on a traditional Welsh melody used for several different folksongs including "Can Mlynedd i 'nawr" ("A hundred years from now").

The legend

Smith is said to have written "Immortal, Invisible" after a mystical experience on the shore near Aberdeen.

OUR STORY

When was the first time you heard this hymn?
What do you recall about that time?

You may need to adapt these questions for the participants in your group. Ask them to record their responses and then share their stories. *(10 minutes)*

What personal memories do you associate with this hymn?

What does this hymn say to you?

THE BIBLICAL STORY

Invite participants to find the passages in their Bibles and record responses to the questions.

Immortal, invisible
1 Timothy 1:17

Why do you think W. Chalmers Smith began his hymn with this image from 1 Timothy?

To all, life thou givest
Nehemiah 9:6

What does it mean to you that life is a gift from God?

In all life thou livest
Acts 17: 24-28

What does this phrase from the hymn declare about God? Do you believe this is true? How does this statement contrast with the text from Timothy?

We blossom and flourish like leaves
Isaiah 40:6-8

What does the hymn say about human life?

Determine if your group would prefer to:

◆ read and respond to all passages and questions before talking

◆ read, respond, and discuss one passage at a time

(20 minutes)

But naught changeth thee
Isaiah 54:10

How does this knowledge affect your life?

LIVING THE STORY

Invite participants to reflect for a few moments on today's conversation, then respond to the questions. It is important to share the responses to these questions, so your group can offer prayer support to each other throughout the week.

Select a leader for your next meeting and remind everyone of the time and location.

Close by singing "Immortal, Invisible" and praying together.

(10 minutes)

What does this hymn say to you at this time in your life?

How does this hymn affect the way you live each day?

Are there specific times this week when you might live your response to this hymn?

O Ancient of Days, you are most blessed,
   most glorious, and deserving of praise.
Fill your people with awe and love
   in your splendid presence.
Rule in might and justice and the light of wisdom.
Remember your people and hear our prayers.
Silence for reflection.
All honor and glory are yours forever and ever.
Amen

HOLY, HOLY, HOLY

1 Ho - ly, ho - ly, ho - ly, Lord God Al - might - y!
2 Ho - ly, ho - ly, ho - ly! All the saints a - dore thee,
3 Ho - ly, ho - ly, ho - ly! Though the dark - ness hide thee,
4 Ho - ly, ho - ly, ho - ly! Lord God Al - might - y!

Ear - ly in the morn - ing our song shall rise to thee.
cast - ing down their gold - en crowns a - round the glass - y sea;
though the eye made blind by sin thy glo - ry may not see,
All thy works shall praise thy name in earth and sky and sea.

Ho - ly, ho - ly, ho - ly, mer - ci - ful and might - y!
cher - u - bim and ser - a - phim fall - ing down be - fore thee,
on - ly thou art ho - ly; there is none be - side thee,
Ho - ly, ho - ly, ho - ly, mer - ci - ful and might - y!

God in three Per - sons, bless - ed Trin - i - ty!
which wert and art, and ev - er - more shalt be.
per - fect in pow'r, in love and pu - ri - ty.
God in three Per - sons, bless - ed Trin - i - ty!

Text: Reginald Heber, 1783–1826, alt.
Music: NICAEA, John B. Dykes, 1823–1876

GATHERING FOR THE STORY

Greet participants as they arrive. Invite them to record their responses to this question in their book.

Begin with introductions. Ask volunteers to share their definitions of holy, and then say the prayer together.

Invite the group to sing "Holy, Holy, Holy" (see page 6).

(10 minutes)

When you were a child, how did you imagine God? How do you imagine God now? How does this inform your definition of the word holy?

Holy God,
Holy and mighty,
Holy and immortal,
adoration and praise are yours
    from our hearts and minds.
Cherubim and seraphim and all your works
    praise your name.
May our songs rise to you now from this place
    as we your people gather in your name.
Amen

HOLY, HOLY, HOLY

Holy, holy, holy, Lord God Almighty!
Early in the morning our song shall rise to thee.
Holy, holy, holy, merciful and mighty!
God in three Persons, blessed Trinity!

Holy, holy, holy! All the saints adore thee,
casting down their golden crowns
around the glassy sea;
cherubim and seraphim falling down before thee,
which wert and art and evermore shalt be.

Holy, holy, holy! Though the darkness hide thee,
though the eye made blind by sin
thy glory may not see,
only thou art holy; there is none beside thee,
perfect in pow'r, in love and purity.

Holy, holy, holy! Lord God Almighty!
All thy works shall praise thy name
in earth and sky and sea.
Holy, holy, holy, merciful and mighty!
God in three Persons, blessed Trinity!

Text: Reginald Heber, 1783-1826, alt.

LEARNING THE STORY

After participants read the hymn background, talk about information they found meaningful or helpful.
(5 minutes)

The text

Reginald Heber, who desired to weave together the sermon, the hymns, and the liturgy in the worship services of the Anglican church, collected and commissioned hymns for each Sunday in the church year. He contributed the hymn "Holy, Holy, Holy," a metrical paraphrase of Revelation 4:8-11 appointed for Trinity Sunday, first published in 1827 in his *Hymns Written and Adapted to the Weekly Church Services of the Year*. Heber was born in Malpas, Cheshire, England, on April 21, 1783. During his service as Vicar of Hodnet, Shropshire, he wrote most of his hymn texts, including "Brightest and Best of the Sons of the Morning" and "From Greenland's Icy Mountains." In 1823 he was appointed bishop of Calcutta. He died suddenly in Trichinopoly, India on April 3, 1826.

The tune

The hymn tune NICAEA, composed by John Bacchus Dykes (1823-1876), first appeared in *Hymns Ancient and Modern* (1859-61). Dykes appears to have based his melody on the 1850 tune TRINITY by John Hopkins and named it for the Council of Nicaea in 325 at which the doctrine of the Trinity, God proclaimed as three persons—Father, Son, and Holy Spirit—was set forth. A child prodigy who began to play the organ at his grandfather's church at the age of 10, he received the Bachelor of Arts degree from St. Catherine's College, Cambridge, where he helped found the University Music Society. During his lifetime he composed almost 300 hymn tunes. Dykes died at the age of 53 in 1876.

The legend

Alfred Lord Tennyson is said to have viewed "Holy, Holy, Holy" as the finest hymn ever written in English.

OUR STORY

When was the first time you heard this hymn?
What do you recall about that time?

You may need to adapt these questions for the participants in your group. Ask them to record their responses and then share their stories. *(10 minutes)*

What personal memories do you associate with this hymn?

What does this hymn say to you?

THE BIBLICAL STORY

Invite participants to find the passages in their Bibles and record responses to the questions.

Holy, holy, holy
Isaiah 6:3

Why do you think the writer of Isaiah used the word holy three times? Why might Reginald Heber have done so in his hymn?

Our song shall rise to thee
Revelation 4:8

How does our song fit into the scene depicted in Revelation?

Casting down their golden crowns
Revelation 4:9-11

Why do the elders cast down their crowns?

Determine if your group would prefer to:

◆ read and respond to all passages and questions before talking

◆ read, respond, and discuss one passage at a time

(20 minutes)

Which wert and art and evermore shall be
Revelation 4:8

What seems to be the quality of God most esteemed by the writer of this hymn?

LIVING THE STORY

Invite participants to reflect for a few moments on today's conversation, then respond to the questions. It is important to share the responses to these questions so your group can offer prayer support to each other throughout the week.

Since this is the last session, take a few minutes to talk about future study this group might want to pursue.

Close by singing, "Holy, Holy, Holy," or you may wish to sing all five hymns from *The Presence of God*.

(10 minutes)

What does this hymn say to you at this time in your life?

How does this hymn affect the way you live each day?

Are there specific times this week when you might live your response to this hymn?

Holy are you, O Lord our God,
    and holy is your name.
You are perfect in power, perfect in love,
    perfect in purity.
Make perfect in us your will, that we may praise
    you in our songs and in our lives.
Boldly we let our prayers rise to you.
Silence for reflection.
May our songs rise as pure and adoring praise,
    to the glory of your holy name.
Amen

RESOURCES

Compact Discs

Hymn ("Holy, Holy, Holy," track 13). The American Boy Choir; James Litton; Music Director. To order, go to http://www.americanboychoir.org/recordingspage.htm

St. Olaf Choir: Great Hymns of Faith ("Great is Thy Faithfulness," track 2). The St. Olaf Choir; Anton Armstrong, conductor. To order, call 507-646-3646 or e-mail music@stolaf.edu

Piano Arrangements

Around the World: Six Hymn Tune Improvisations ("Immortal, Invisible, God Only Wise"), Mark Dorian. Augsburg Fortress Publishers (ISBN 0-8006-5494-3). To order, call 1-800-328-4648 or go to www.augsburgfortress.org/store

Blessed Assurance: A Piano Collection ("What a Fellowship, What a Joy Divine," "Blessed Assurance"), J. Bert Carlson. Augsburg Fortress Publishers (ISBN 0-8006-5804-3). To order, call 1-800-328-4648 or go to www.augsburgfortress.org/store

Crystal Tide and Falling Stars: Contemporary Music of Praise Stylized for Piano ("Blessed Assurance"), Peter Ramsey. Augsburg Fortress Publishers (ISBN 0-8006-5493-5). To order, call 1-800-328-4648 or go to www.augsburgfortress.org/store

It is Well With My Soul: Sacred Piano Solos ("Great is Thy Faithfulness"), Pam Gervais. Augsburg Fortress Publishers (ISBN 0-8006-7476-6). To order, call 1-800-328-4648 or go to www.augsburgfortress.org/store

Jazz Sunday Morning: Piano Arrangements ("What a Fellowship, What a Joy Divine," "Blessed Assurance"), Michael Hassell. Augsburg Fortress Publishers (ISBN 0-8006-5540-0). To order, call 1-800-328-4648 or go to www.augsburgfortress.org/store

Let it Rip! At the Piano: Congregational Song Accompaniments for Piano ("What a Fellowship, What a Joy Divine," "Blessed Assurance"). Augsburg Fortress Publishers (ISBN 0-8006-5906-6). To order, call 1-800-328-4648 or go to www.augsburgfortress.org/store